The instant she got back from vacation,
Zelda Zink phoned her best friend Mimi Mink…

and said, "Can you drop by this afternoon?
You can bring your toy poodle, Fifi La Frink."

You see, Zelda had a great gift for her pal:
a souvenir T-shirt from the Island of Tink.

But before her guests arrived,
Zelda spilled a bottle—
covering the shirt with PURPLE ink!

Quick as a wink,
she scrubbed the shirt
with some toothpaste
she found by the sink.

And the ink disappeared,
but now the shirt
had a peppermint stink!

6

Quick as a wink,
she doused it with cherry drink.
And the smell disappeared,
but the shirt turned bright pink!

Quick as a wink,
she tossed it in the washer and dryer.
And the pink disappeared,
but did that shirt ever shrink!

"Clink! Clink!" went the doorbell.
Oh no—it's Mimi Mink!

They hugged hello, then Mimi asked:
"What's that teeny T-shirt
from the Island of Tink?"

What to do? What to do?
Zelda had to think.
"I brought it back from vacation...
isn't it perfect for... Fifi La Frink?"

"Why, that is soooooo precious!"
squealed Mimi Mink.
The tears of joy made her blink.

Then Mimi put the T-shirt on Fifi La Frink
who barked a BIG thank you to dear Zelda Zink—
who was now rather happy she spilled purple ink!

Listen to the riddle sentences. Add the right letter or letters to the -ink sound to finish each one.

1 I brush my teeth at the bathroom ___ink.

2 When you are thirsty, you should have a ___ink.

3 I like the color blue. My sister likes ___ink.

4 Let's all go ice-skating at the ___ink.

5 When you open and close both eyes quickly, you ___ink.

6 If you close and open one eye quickly, you're giving a ___ink.

7 My change dropped in the piggy bank with a ____ink.

8 The balloon was slowly losing air and starting to _____ink.

9 Your brain is the thing that helps you ____ink.

10 When a skunk gets scared it makes quite a ____ink.

> Now make up some new riddle sentences using -ink

-ink Cheer

Give a great holler, a cheer, a yell

For all of the words that we can spell

With an I, N, and K that make the sound –ink,

You'll find it in pink and mink and think.

Three little letters, that's all that we need

To make a whole family of words to read!

Make a list of other –ink words. Then use them in the cheer!